About the Cover: The African crocodile and the little crocodile bird are very unusual partners. The crocodile is a fierce animal with powerful, quick-moving jaws. But it lets the little bird sit on its back and eat insects that annoy it. It even opens its mouth to let the bird find worms and insects among its sharp teeth.

Wonders of Nature

A Random House PICTUREBACK®

It is a wonder
of nature that
the wolf, with its
keen sense of smell,
does not notice the little
fawn hidden in the grass.
Fawns are born with no
scent at all, so their enemies
have trouble finding them.

Wonders
of Nature

by Walter Linsenmaier

RANDOM HOUSE 🏠 NEW YORK

Library of Congress Cataloging in Publication Data: Linsenmaier, Walter. Wonders of nature. SUMMARY: Presents unusual facts about a number of different animals, including the metamorphosis of a butterfly, the unusual nests some birds build, and unique defense mechanisms. 1. Zoology—Miscellanea—Juvenile literature. [1. Animals— Miscellanea] I. Title. QL49.L75 591 78-62133 ISBN: 0-394-84083-6 (B.C.); 0-394-84091-7 (trade); 0-394-94091-1 (lib. bdg.)

Manufactured in the United States of America   A B C D E F G H I J K   3 4 5 6 7 8 9 0

The bullfrog lives part of its life in the water and part of it on land. A full-grown North American bullfrog can be as long as eighteen inches from the tip of its nose to the ends of its hind feet. But the bullfrog is not always that large.

The female lays hundreds of eggs in the water. When the eggs hatch in a few weeks, tiny tadpoles, or polliwogs, come out and cling to water plants. The tadpoles look like little fish as they begin to swim about, eating very small plants.

As a tadpole gets larger it starts to grow legs. It also grows lungs for breathing air. Finally its tail begins to shrink. The tadpole changes into a baby bullfrog and goes to live on the land. This change is called metamorphosis. It is one of the most remarkable wonders of nature.

Butterflies also go through the change called metamorphosis. They must go through several changes before they can fly about.

The mourning cloak butterfly starts its life as a tiny egg on the branch of a tree. When the egg hatches, a hungry little caterpillar comes out. The little caterpillar almost never stops gobbling leaves.

The caterpillar grows so quickly that its soft skin becomes too small. The skin splits open several times and the caterpillar wriggles out, covered with a new and larger skin.

When the caterpillar is fully grown, it stops eating and attaches itself to a branch. It hangs head down and sheds its skin once again. The next skin is harder than the others. Now the caterpillar is called a chrysalis.

Inside the hard skin something wonderful happens. The caterpillar's body changes. It grows antennae and wings. When the new creature breaks out of the skin, its wings are folded up. But within a few hours the wings spread out and a mourning cloak butterfly flies away.

Some animals are protected from danger because they look like other animals.
The death's-head moth looks a lot like a wasp. It can also make a chirping
sound and twitch its head and fat body. Many animals, such as the dormouse,
are afraid to eat a wasp. So they won't go near the death's-head moth.

The fairy tern lives near the coast of the Indian Ocean. It is the only bird that dares to hatch its single egg high up on a branch without a nest.

There are almost as many different kinds of nests as there are birds that build them. The robin smooths out its nest with mud. The hummingbird softens its bowl-shaped nest by lining it with bits of fluffy plant down. The Baltimore oriole weaves a large hanging pouch. And the crested swift of Indonesia glues a nutshell-like nest made of bark and feathers to the branch of a tree.

The flying lizard and the flying frog cannot really fly.
But they can glide for great distances from tree to tree.
    The flying lizard spreads out the folds of skin along its body
like wings. It looks like a colorful butterfly as it glides to
another tree several hundred feet away. Here a male lizard is
visiting his mate. Flying lizards live in the woods of Indonesia
and grow to be about eight inches long.

The flying frog has a flying skin between its toes. It can glide to another tree up to fifty feet away. This little frog lives in Asia and grows to a length of three inches.

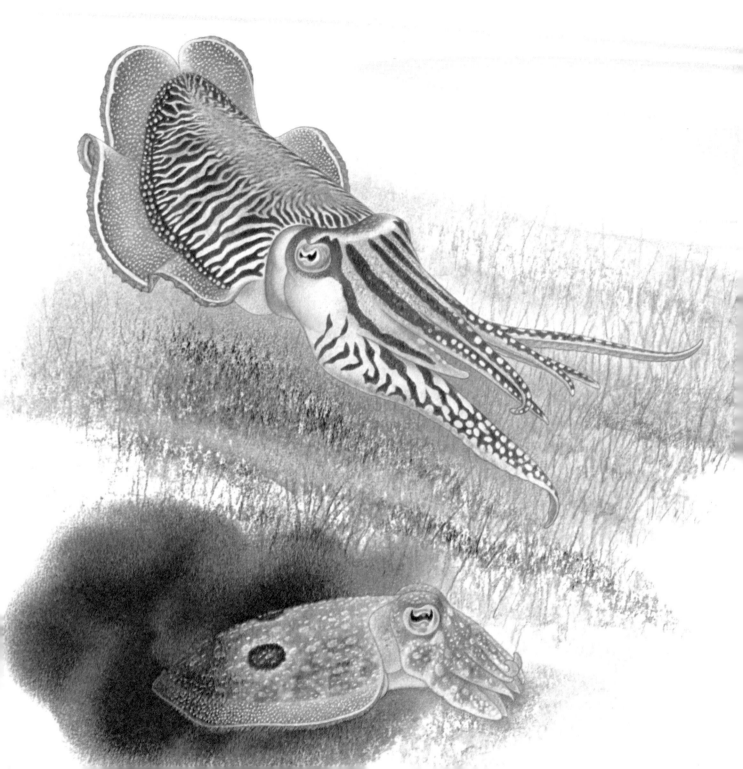

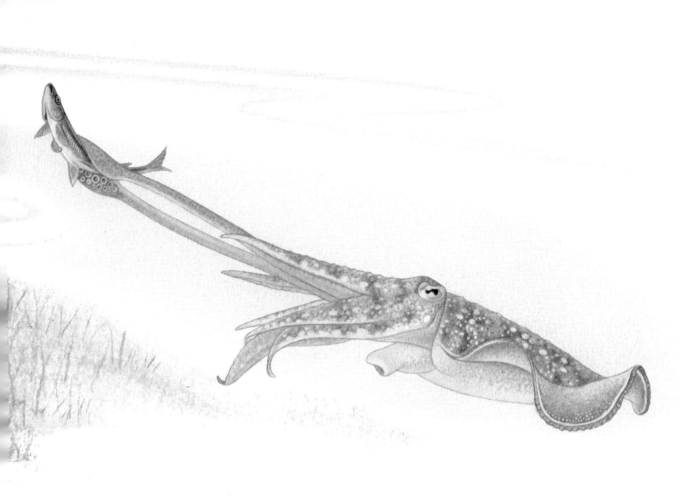

These cuttlefish are not really fish at all. They are a kind of squid. Cuttlefish live at the bottom of the sea in the shallow water near the shore. When a cuttlefish is frightened, it blows water out through its breathing tube and zooms away backward. It can also squirt out a black ink called sepia. The ink makes a cloud in the water that hides the cuttlefish from its enemies.

Cuttlefish have ten arms, but they keep two long ones hidden away. If a cuttlefish spots a shrimp or a fish, its two hidden arms quickly shoot out to grab the food.

Puffer fish are small, slow swimmers, but they have a wonderful way to protect themselves from danger. If a bird grabs a puffer, the fish swallows air and blows itself up. Then the bird cannot hold it.

If a bigger fish comes near, the puffer quickly puffs itself up by swallowing water, scaring the big fish away.

The little archerfish lives in India.
It eats insects and spiders. When it
sees an insect above the water, it spits
out drops of water and knocks the insect
down. The archerfish can shoot an insect
up to twenty-five inches away.

The chameleon is a remarkable creature. It changes its color so that it blends in with the bushes around it. This lizard can change color when it is angry or scared, when the weather is cold or hot, and when it is in darkness or sunlight. It always has a perfect disguise.

Many kinds of chameleons live in Africa. They creep very slowly among the bushes. Their necks are short, so they cannot turn their heads. But they can move each of their eyes in a different direction. A chameleon can look forward and backward at the same time.

The chameleon catches insects with its long, sticky tongue. That tongue moves so quickly it's hard to see it.

When the Australian frilled lizard is in danger, it stands up on its hind legs and runs away very fast. Even the quick-moving, catlike dasyure has trouble catching it.

The frilled lizard can also frighten its enemies away. It stands up, unfolds the loose skin around its neck, opens its mouth, and hisses. It looks as fierce as a dragon— much fiercer than it really is.

The frilled lizard may grow up to thirty-two inches long and its collar can measure nine inches across.

Many animals never see their young. Butterflies and frogs are some of these. Other animals take care of their babies for long periods of time. A baby monkey clings to its mother's fur from the moment it is born. It may stay with its mother until it is a year or two old.

Some animals look quite different from their mothers. In a few years the reddish-blond baby monkey will grow up to look like its mother.

But the panther's baby will not look like its mother. A black panther is really an all-black leopard. It often has babies that grow up with the same bright-yellow, spotted coats that most leopards have.

Except for humans, the great apes are the most intelligent animals on earth. Gorillas are the largest apes. The gorilla mother gives her baby a lot of love and attention. The games she plays with the baby help it grow up agile and strong. Though gorillas look fierce, they are really quite shy. They live in the forests of Africa and eat tender green plants.

Most birds are good mothers,
but not the European cuckoo. She
lays her egg in the nest of some
other bird. Then the cuckoo
mother flies away while the other
bird sits on her egg.

When the baby cuckoo hatches,
it is usually bigger than the other
babies in the nest.

This baby cuckoo has grown even
bigger than the goldfinch mother
who is feeding it. But the goldfinch
doesn't seem to mind. She'll go
on feeding the baby cuckoo
until it is big enough to fly away.

The mother grebe carries her babies
for a long time on her warm back.

Male and female hornbills
are most unusual parents.
They find a tree with a hollow
in it and the female climbs in.
Together they close up the opening
with mud, leaving only a tiny hole.

The female hornbill stays in her dark dungeon
for up to four months. She lays one egg, sometimes
two, and sits on it until it hatches. Her mate spends
all of his time bringing food to her and the new baby.

When the young hornbill is bigger, the mother hacks her way out of the hollow and goes out to help with the feeding. By this time she is fat and has grown a new set of feathers. Her mate is thin and worn out from all of his hard work.

Meanwhile, the youngster closes the hole once again and stays in the hollow until it is big enough to fly away.

Scientists don't know very much about the animals that live at the
bottom of the ocean. But those they know about are true wonders
of nature. The electric eel can give its enemies a powerful shock.
The deep-sea angler has a kind of fishing rod growing out of its head.
When other fish come near, the angler eats them. The long,
slithery oarfish is one of the few deep-sea
creatures that sometimes swim to the top.

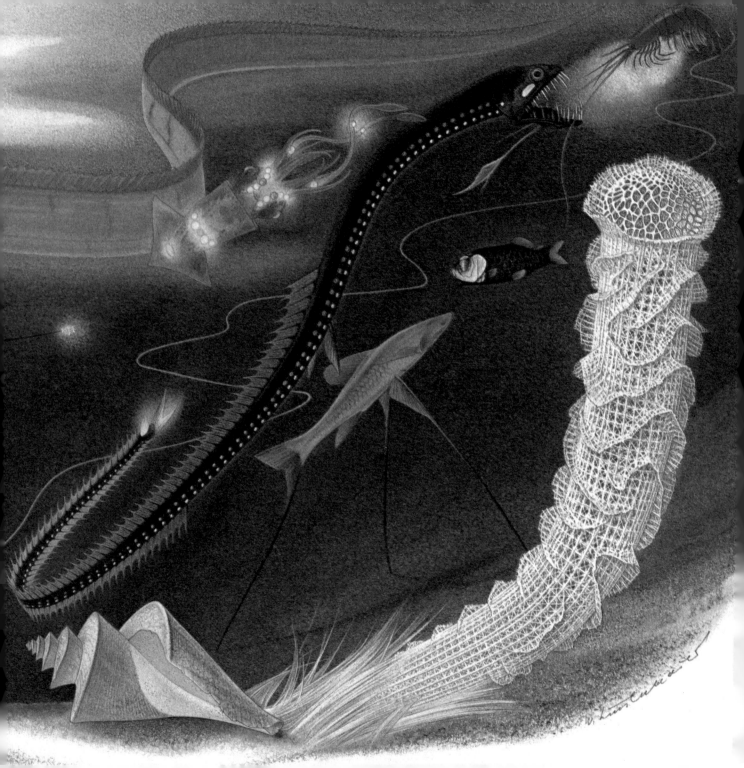

In the winter when it is cold and there seems to be no life outdoors, all kinds of animals are living under the ice and snow. A chrysalis hangs from a bush. In the spring a swallowtail butterfly will come out of it. A ground beetle and some milkweed bugs are hidden under moss and stones. A sulphur butterfly hides under dry leaves. A painted lady butterfly is sleeping in the hollow tree. Burrowed in the bark are some ladybird beetles and a bumblebee. A spotted salamander sleeps under the roots. All of these animals will come alive when spring arrives.

The snowshoe hare is usually brown. But when cold weather comes it sheds its coat and grows a thick, warm, snow-white one. This new coat helps the hare hide from its enemies.

Scientists know about more than a million kinds of animals. And each one is a wonder of nature in its own way.